SHAPE

SHUFFLE

SHAPE
SHUFFLE

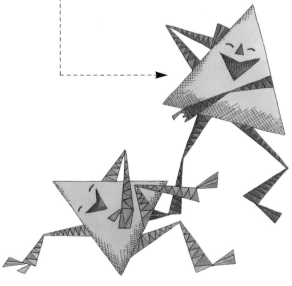

WORLD BOOK, INC.

CHICAGO LONDON SYDNEY TORONTO

World Book, Inc.
525 W. Monroe
Chicago, IL 60661
U.S.A.

Editor: Melissa Tucker
Design: Lisa Buckley
Cover design: Design 5

Library of Congress Cataloging-in-Publication Data

Shape shuffle.
        p.   cm. -- (World Book's mind benders)
    Summary: A collection of puzzles challenging the reader to make shapes and designs out of toothpicks, coins, or buttons and then change the shapes in various ways.
    ISBN 0-7166-4107-0 (softcover)
    1. Geometry--Juvenile literature. 2. Mathematical recreations--Juvenile literature [1. Shape. 2. Geometry. 3. Puzzles. 4. Mathematical recreations.] I. World Book, Inc. II. Series.
    QA445.5.S497 1997
    793.7'4--dc21   97-6016

For information on other World Book products, call 1-800-255-1750, X2238, or visit us at our Web site at http://www.worldbook.com

Printed in Singapore.

1 2 3 4 5 99 98 97

Introduction

The puzzles in this book show you how to make shapes and designs out of toothpicks, coins, or buttons. Then you have to change the shapes to something else. To make the change, you just shuffle, or move, the coins or toothpicks around until you have the right shape.

Sounds easy? Don't be too sure! Sometimes, it will seem that you just *can't* change the shape the way the puzzle tells you to! But keep trying—it can be done. And, be sure to read each puzzle carefully, because sometimes there's a clue hidden in what the puzzle says.

The spilled ice cream

Arrange two toothpicks and a large coin or button like this:

Think of this shape as an ice-cream cone with one scoop of ice cream in it. Can you move one toothpick so that the ice-cream cone is upside down and the ice cream (the coin) is no longer inside the cone?

(ANSWER ON PAGE 28)

House into squares

Using six toothpicks, make a "house" like this:

Now, moving only two toothpicks, change the "house" into five squares.

(ANSWER ON PAGE 28)

Seeing squares

How many squares do you see?

(ANSWER ON PAGE 28)

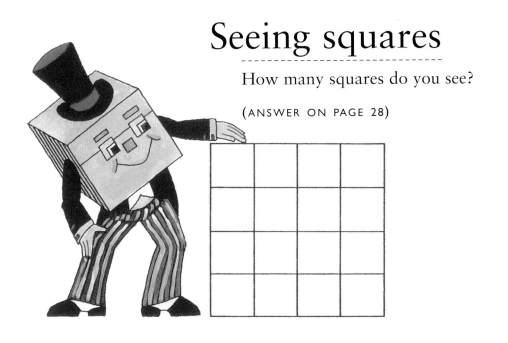

Seeing triangles

This square has been divided into triangles.
How many triangles can you find?

(ANSWER ON PAGE 28)

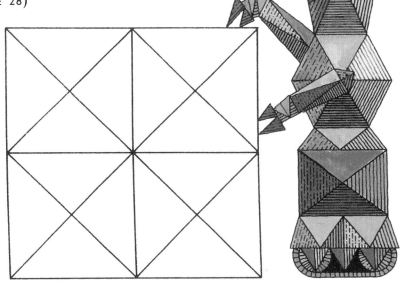

Turn the fish

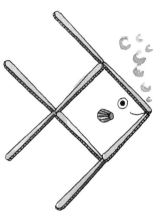

Arrange eight toothpicks to make a "tropical fish," as shown at left.

When you finish, the fish will be swimming to your right. Can you turn it around, so it's swimming to your left? But to do this, you may move only three toothpicks!

(ANSWER ON PAGE 28)

A toothpick creature

With thirteen toothpicks, make a toothpick creature like the one shown here.

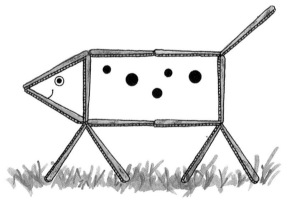

The toothpick creature is looking to your left. Can you make it look to the right, by moving only two of the toothpicks? (This is tricky!)

(ANSWER ON PAGE 28)

The Chubbs and Slimms

With eighteen toothpicks, make two "houses" and a "yard" as shown below. Place four buttons, as shown, for "trees."

The house on the left belongs to the Chubb family. The house on the right belongs to the Slimm family. Each family owns half the yard. But they can't figure out how to divide it so that each family will have two trees. Using no more than three toothpicks, build a fence that will divide the yard into two equal parts, with two trees in each part.

(ANSWER ON PAGE 28)

A toothpick jail

With four toothpicks, make a square, as shown above. Put three small buttons or coins inside the square, as shown.

The square is a "jail," and the buttons or coins are "prisoners." But each prisoner must be in a separate cell. Using two more toothpicks, but without letting any toothpicks cross each other, make "walls" inside the jail so that each prisoner is in a separate cell.

(ANSWER ON PAGE 28)

Ice-cream sundae

Arrange four toothpicks and a small button or coin this way:

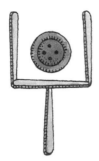

This is an ice-cream sundae glass with a cherry in it! Can you turn the glass upside down and get the cherry out by moving only two toothpicks?

(ANSWER ON PAGE 29)

Triangle teasers

An *equilateral* (ee kwuh lat uhr uhl) triangle is a triangle that has three equal sides. It's easy to make an equilateral triangle with three toothpicks. You just put them together like this:

It's also easy to make five equilateral triangles out of fifteen toothpicks.

But—

1. Can you make *five* equilateral triangles out of only *nine* toothpicks? (Here's a hint—the triangles don't all have to be the same size.)

2. Can you make *six* equilateral triangles using only *six* toothpicks? (No, you can't break any of the toothpicks in two!)

3. Can you make *eight* equilateral triangles with only *six* toothpicks? It can be done!

A triangle doesn't have to be equilateral, with all sides equal, of course. It can have two sides equal and one side different, as shown at right. This kind of triangle is called an *isosceles* (eye sahs uh leez) triangle.

4. Using three toothpicks, make an isosceles triangle with two open angles at the bottom corners, like this:

Can you add two more toothpicks so as to make a total of ten triangles? Here's a hint—some triangles will be inside others.

(ANSWERS ON PAGE 29)

Square stuff

For each of the first four puzzles, arrange twelve toothpicks to make four squares, as shown at left.

1. Take away two toothpicks from the four squares, so that only two squares are left.

2. Take away four toothpicks from the four squares. Now, put them back so that there are three squares, all the same size.

3. Take away three toothpicks from the four squares. Now, put them back so there are three squares, all the same size.

4. Now, arrange the twelve toothpicks to form seven squares. (Here's a hint—all the squares won't be the same size.)

For each of the next two puzzles, arrange seventeen toothpicks to make six squares, like this:

5. Take five toothpicks from the six squares so that only three squares, all the same size, are left.

6. Take six toothpicks from the six squares so that only two squares are left.

For each of the next three puzzles, arrange twenty-four toothpicks into nine squares, like this:

7. Take four toothpicks from the nine squares so that only five squares, all the same size, are left.

8. Take eight toothpicks from the nine squares so that only five squares, all the same size, are left.

9. Take eight toothpicks from the nine squares so that only two squares are left.

10. For this puzzle, arrange eleven toothpicks to make three squares, as shown at left. By moving three toothpicks, change the three squares into two squares.

11. For this puzzle, arrange sixteen toothpicks to make five squares, like this:

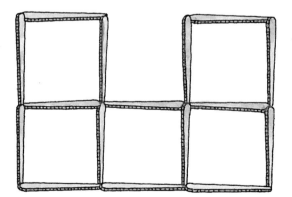

By moving three toothpicks, change the five squares into four squares, all the same size.

12. For this puzzle, arrange twenty toothpicks to make seven squares, like this:

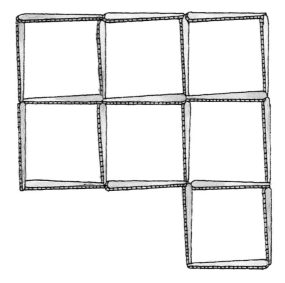

By moving three toothpicks, change the seven squares into five squares, all the same size.

(ANSWERS ON PAGE 30)

Six squares

Arrange twelve toothpicks to form a large square, as shown at right. Now, can you take eight more toothpicks and make six squares inside the large square?

(ANSWER ON PAGE 30)

Tricky tasks

These puzzles are real foolers! You must think hard about what you have to do. But, once you figure them out, you can have a lot of fun fooling your friends with them.

1. Place six toothpicks in a row, an equal distance apart, like this:

   Now, add five more toothpicks in a way that will make NINE!

2. Arrange twelve toothpicks to form three squares.

   By taking away three toothpicks, and rearranging others, it is possible to make TEN!

3. Arrange sixteen toothpicks in four squares.

   Believe it or not, by taking away two toothpicks and rearranging others, you can actually end up with NONE!

(ANSWERS ON PAGE 31)

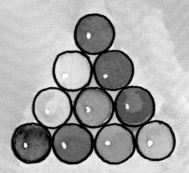

Triangle turnaround

Using buttons or coins, set up a triangle like the one shown here. Then, by moving only *three* of the buttons, see if you can turn the whole triangle around to face the other way, with the point at the bottom!

(ANSWER ON PAGE 31)

Three in a row

1. Lay three pennies or other coins in a row. The middle coin should be tails up. The other coins should be heads up. Turning over only one coin at a time, make all three coins heads up in three moves.

2. Lay three coins in a row, as before, with the middle one tails up and the other two heads up. Turning over two coins at a time, make all the coins tails up in three moves.

3. Lay three coins in a row. Change the position of the middle coin—that is, get it out of the middle—without touching it!

(ANSWERS ON PAGE 31)

The farmer

Arrange eight toothpicks like this:

1. A prosperous farmer had a piece of land that was this shape. He wanted to divide the land into six equal parts, because he planned to grow a different crop in each part. Using five more toothpicks, can you divide the land into six equal parts?

2. One day, the farmer decided that he ought to have a will. So, he went to see his lawyer. The farmer told the lawyer that when he died, he wanted to leave one-third of his land to his wife. He wanted another third divided into two equal parts for his two sons. And he wanted to divide the last third into four equal parts for his four grandchildren.

   Using the five toothpicks you used to divide the farmer's land into six parts, can you show the lawyer how to divide the land the way the farmer wants to do it?

(ANSWERS ON PAGE 32)

One, not two

For this puzzle, you will need five toothpicks and four coins. Arrange the toothpicks in the shape of a five-pointed star, as shown at right.

Start at any toothpick. Moving clockwise, count three toothpicks. Put a coin at the end of the third toothpick.

Do this four times until four of the toothpicks have a coin. But, here's the catch—you may *never* start from a toothpick that has a coin. And you can't leave two coins at a toothpick.

(ANSWER ON PAGE 32)

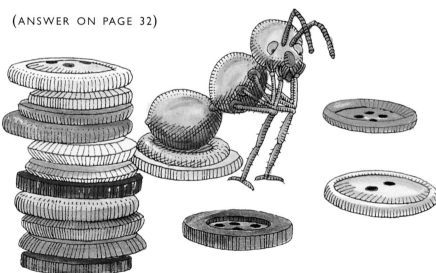

Rows and rows

Can you arrange sixteen buttons so that they form ten rows with four buttons in each row and four rows with three buttons in each row?

(ANSWER ON PAGE 32)

Can it be done?

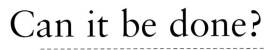

1. It's easy to arrange fifteen buttons in five rows with three buttons in each row.

But can you arrange *seven* buttons in five rows with three buttons in each row?

2. It's easy to arrange twenty buttons in five rows with four buttons in each row. But can you arrange *ten* buttons in five rows with four buttons in each row?

(ANSWERS ON PAGE 32)

The mouse king's treasure

The king of the mice had a treasury. It was a big room, full of all kinds of cheese! He kept the room locked, of course. And he kept the key on a tiny island surrounded by a deep, eight-sided moat. In the moat swam deadly sharp-toothed sharks.

When the king wanted some cheese, he had his mouseketeer guards carry a small boat down to the moat. He rowed out to the island, got the key, and rowed back. When the boat wasn't in use, it was kept locked away.

The king felt sure that none of his subjects could ever get the key to the cheese treasury. But, one night, a rascally mouse by the name of Cheeky managed to steal the key! He did this using only two toothpicks.

On the opposite page, there is a picture of the moat and island. It is the same size as the king's moat and island. Using two toothpicks, see if you can figure out how Cheeky got across the moat. But remember, the toothpicks must not touch the water.

(ANSWER ON PAGE 32)

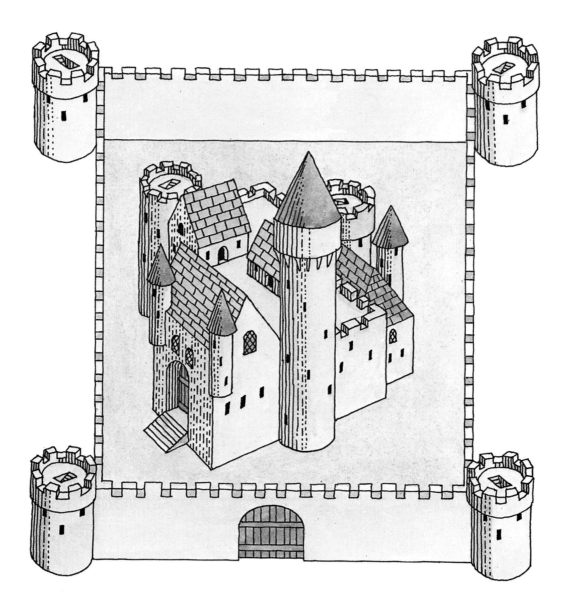

Baron Baddguy's wall

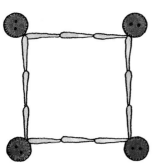

The castle of Baron Baddguy is surrounded by a square wall. At each corner of the wall there is a round tower. To make a plan of the wall and towers, arrange twelve toothpicks and four buttons, as shown at left.

Baron Baddguy wants to double the space inside the wall. But he wants the wall to be square and he wants to keep the four towers just where they are, on the outside of the wall. Can you show him how to do this?

You can use the twelve toothpicks, plus four more. You may move the toothpicks any way you wish. But the new wall must form a square and it must enclose twice as much space as the old wall. The four towers can't be moved, and must be outside the new wall.

(ANSWER ON PAGE 32)

Answers

The spilled ice cream (PAGE 6)

To turn the cone upside down, simply move one of the toothpicks to the right (or left), as shown.

House into squares (PAGE 6)

Move the two toothpicks that form the roof so as to make a cross inside the square, as shown. This makes four small squares inside one large square, or a total of five squares.

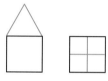

Seeing squares (PAGE 7)

There is one large square with sixteen small squares inside it, making seventeen. But ...

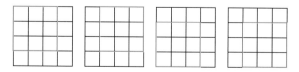

the small squares can be combined like this to make nine more squares, or a total of twenty-six squares. And...

the small squares can be combined in other ways to form four slightly larger squares. So, altogether, there are thirty squares.

Seeing triangles (PAGE 7)

There are forty-four triangles in all, as shown below.

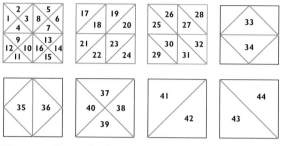

Turn the fish (PAGE 8)

The three toothpicks that must be moved to make the fish change direction are shown in blue.

A toothpick creature (PAGE 8)

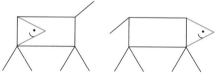

The Chubbs and Slimms
(PAGE 9)

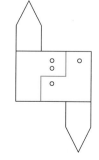

A toothpick jail (PAGE 10)

Ice-cream sundae (PAGE 11)

To turn the glass upside down, first slide the horizontal toothpick over, as shown in (b) below.

   Then move the leftover toothpick to form the other side of the glass, as shown in (c).

Triangle teasers (PAGE 12)

1. To make five equilateral triangles with nine toothpicks, arrange the nine toothpicks to form four equilateral triangles, as shown below.

   These four triangles form one large triangle, making five triangles in all.

2. To make six equilateral triangles with only six toothpicks, first make one triangle with three toothpicks, as in (a). Next, make a second triangle with the other three toothpicks, and place it point down on top of the first triangle, as shown in (b).

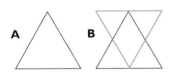

   You now have four small equilateral triangles at each corner, plus the two large triangles, for a total of six.

3. To make eight equilateral triangles, place one three-toothpick triangle over another one, like this:

   This gives you two small triangles, one at the top and one at the bottom, and four smaller ones, two on each side. That's a total of eight, counting the two you started with.

4. To make ten triangles from one isosceles triangle, add the two toothpicks as shown.

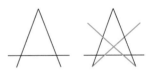

   Here are the ten triangles this forms:

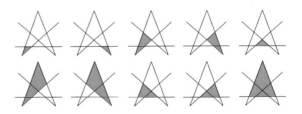

   It is also possible to make ten triangles by placing two toothpicks this way:

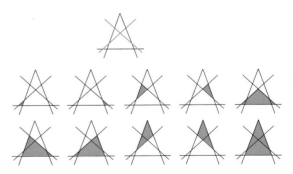

Answers

Square stuff (PAGE 14)

The toothpicks that were taken away, or moved, are shown in blue.

1.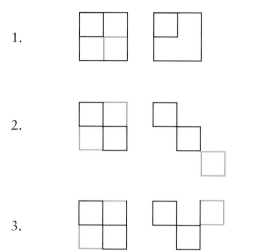

2.

3.

4. To form seven squares with twelve toothpicks, arrange two squares of four toothpicks each, with the corners touching, as shown in (a).

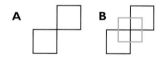

Lay a third four-toothpick square over the other two squares, as shown in (b). This forms four smaller squares, for a total of seven.

5.

6.

7.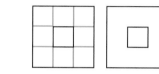

8.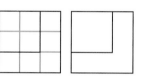

9.

or

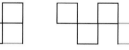

10.

11.

12.

Six squares (PAGE 17)

30

Answers

Tricky tasks (PAGE 18)

1. To add five toothpicks to the six and make NINE, place the five toothpicks as shown by the blue lines.

2. Here's how to make TEN out of three squares by taking away three toothpicks and rearranging the others.

3. Here's how to make NONE out of four squares by taking away two toothpicks and rearranging the others.

Triangle turnaround (PAGE 19)

Move the end buttons on the bottom row to the second row. Move the button that's on top to the bottom.

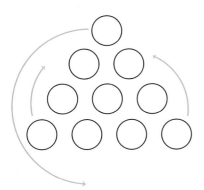

Three in a row (PAGE 20)

1.

(a) Turn over the coin on the right.

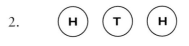

(b) Turn over the coin in the middle.

(c) Turn over the coin on the right.

2.

(a) Turn over the coins on the ends.

(b) Turn over the coin in the middle and the coin on the right.

(c) Turn over the coin in the middle and the coin on the right.

3. Move the coin on the left (or right) so that the middle coin becomes an outside coin without being touched.

Answers

The farmer (PAGE 21)

1. The five toothpicks that divide the shape into six parts are shown in blue.

2. To divide the shape into thirds, place two toothpicks as shown in (a) below.

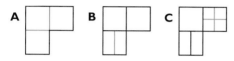

Leave one-third for the farmer's wife. Using one toothpick, divide another third in half for the farmer's sons, as shown in (b).

Divide the last third into four equal parts by placing one toothpick across another as shown in (c).

One, not two (PAGE 22)

The trick is to count in a clockwise direction. Always start with the toothpick that comes after the one by which you have just put a coin.

In the diagram below, (1) shows where you might start counting for your first move. A coin is placed at the third toothpick. Continuing in a clockwise direction, count from the toothpick marked (2), and place another coin. And so on.

Rows and rows (PAGE 22)

Arrange the buttons as shown below.

There are four rows of four buttons each, running from top to bottom. There are four rows of four buttons each, running from left to right. And there are two rows of four buttons running diagonally. That's ten rows.

In addition, there are four other diagonal rows of three buttons each.

Can it be done? (PAGE 23)

1. Arrange the seven buttons as shown at right. This gives you five rows of three buttons, as shown by the blue lines.
2. Arrange the ten buttons as shown. This gives you five rows of four buttons, as shown by the blue lines.

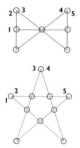

The mouse king's treasure (PAGE 24)

First, Cheeky placed one toothpick across an angle of the pond so that ends rested on the ground. Then he placed the second toothpick with one end resting on the first toothpick and the other end resting on the island, as shown. Thus, he was able to scamper across the second toothpick, get the key, and scamper back.

Baron Baddguy's wall (PAGE 26)

The new wall, made of sixteen toothpicks, is shown in black. The old wall is shown in blue. The new wall encloses exactly twice as much space as the old wall. The towers haven't been moved, and are still outside the wall.

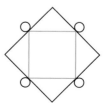